Sharing Christ

W0009377

with Muslims

Sharing Christ with Muslims
a basic guide

ISBN number: 0-9542594-2-4

Published by Frontiers England PO Box 600 Hemel Hempstead HP3 9UG

www.frontiers.org.uk

Introduction

Relationships are important, both to God and to Muslims. Muslims highly value friendships, often more so than Westerners do.

Jesus reached out in love to those outside His culture – to the Samaritan and the Roman – and His love compels us to do likewise. It would be easy for us to focus on obstacles to this; obstacles of history, culture and communication. We can be inhibited by our own fears, prejudices, perhaps ignorance. Do we believe God is already at work in the lives of Muslims and wants to use us in the process?

The obstacles can be overcome. Our lives can be the means of bridging the barriers and communicating Jesus. We hope this book will give you a helpful introduction to building relationships, making friends and sharing the love and blessing of God.

Building friendships with Muslims

Let's start with a few basic pointers:

• Get beyond the labels and stereotypes. See each person first and foremost as someone made in the image of God.

• Acknowledge common ground and enjoy this together. This may be as simple as sharing an interest or pastime. Also acknowledge common values in our respective faiths.

• Genuinely care for the whole person as Jesus did. Demonstrate your interest in their relatives and their health, just as you would with any other friend. Find out their concerns, fears, dreams and aspirations.

• Relationships are two-way. Don't have the attitude "I'm here to give."

• Share about what God has done and is doing in your life. Share graciously and naturally. Don't try to share everything all at once, but be relevant to the heart needs of your friend.

• Be open and honest with your struggles. Later you may be able to share how God has worked in you to overcome weaknesses.

• Be aware that some of the things you may do and words you may use will be understood in a different way.

• Remember that God is in charge of timing. Be natural, be yourself and trust the rest to Him.

• Take time to build friendship. Good friendships don't happen overnight.

Take time to build friendship. Good friendships don't happen overnight

Six beliefs

Any good friendship has a foundation c
to understand one another better. In bu.
relationships with our Muslim friends, it's
have an understanding of what they believe.

In Islam, there are six main beliefs. These are:

God

There is one true God – *Allah* in Arabic – who is entitled to worship and total obedience from human beings.

Angels

The angels are God's servants who reveal His will. The greatest is Gabriel who appeared to Muhammed.

The Prophets

God has spoken through many prophets. The final and greatest was Muhammed. Among the other great prophets were Noah, Abraham, Moses and Jesus.

The Holy Books

The Qur'an is the holiest book of Islam and is considered to be God's final revelation. The Qur'an supersedes all previous revelations including:

Tawrat (the Torah) – given to Moses
Zabur (the Psalms) – given to David
Injil (the Gospel) – given to Jesus

The Day of Judgement

This is the terrible day on which everyone's good deeds will be weighed against their bad deeds to determine whether they go to paradise or hell. Ultimately, none of us can be certain of our fate. It will be God's choice.

The Will of God

God ordains the fate of every creature. A devout Muslim says, 'Inshah Allah' (if Allah wills it) with almost every plan he or she makes.

Five pillars

As well as the six beliefs, there are five pillars which are a Muslim's practical duty. These are:

Affirmation – *Shahada*
The creed 'There is no God but God, and Muhammed is the messenger of God' is repeated constantly by devout Muslims.

The Fast – *Saum*
Muslims are expected to refrain from food, drink, smoking and sex from dawn to sunset every day during the holy month of Ramadan.

Almsgiving – *Zakat*
Muslims are expected to give 2.5% of their income to the poor.

Prayer – *Salat*
Muslims are required to pray set prayers five times a day in a bowing position facing Mecca.

- between dawn and sunrise
- between midday and mid-afternoon
- between mid-afternoon and sunset
- just after sunset
- between nightfall and daybreak

Muslims are required to wash in a special way before praying. Men are expected to attend the mosque for the Friday midday prayers.

Pilgrimage – *Hajj*
All Muslims who can afford it are expected to make a pilgrimage to Mecca at least once in their lifetime.

Diversity among Muslims

Just as in the Christian world there is a wide range of belief and practice, the same is true in Islam. There are around 150 different branches, but they can be divided into two main groups:

Sunni (about 85% of Muslims)

Sunnis try to follow the sayings and actions of Muhammed which were collected after his death in the books of the Hadith. They believe the Hadith show how to put into practice the guidance given in the Qur'an.

Shia (about 15% of Muslims)

Shias (also called Shi'ites) – found mainly in Iran and Iraq – believe that keeping to the straight path and avoiding error comes from following a charismatic and infallible leader, the Imam. They have a non-literal interpretation of the Qur'an and their own collections of Hadith.

There are almost 150 different branches of Islam

Across these divisions, you can also find the following:

Sufis

Between a third and a half of the Muslim world is involved in a Sufi brotherhood. These groups are led by a 'holy man' who gives spiritual guidance in the search for union with God through self-discipline, mystical intuition, and sometimes music and dancing.

Folk Islam

Two thirds of Muslims follow a mixture of Islam and folk religions. Folk Islam is very popular with women who believe it gives them some control of the spirit world. Prayers are often mediated through dead holy men or saints. Belief in evil jinn (spirits) is part of orthodox Islam, but appeasing the jinn is a major focus of folk practice.

Widen your vocabulary

Friendship building is centred around communication. To help you along the way, here are some of the words commonly used by Muslims:

Allah   God – the Supreme Being. Ninety nine 'beautiful names' give some idea of what He is like. The 99 names of God are sometimes recited with the aid of a 33 or 99-bead rosary.

Hadith   The sayings and actions of Muhammed which were collected after his death.

Hajji   Someone who has made the pilgrimage (Hajj) to Mecca.

Id-ul-Fitr   The two major festivals in Islam. Id-ul-Fitr
and   comes at the end of Ramadan. Muslims
Id-ul-Adha visit friends and relatives, eat special food and give presents to children. Id-ul-Adha, about ten weeks later, commemorates Abraham's offering of Ishmael (not Isaac) as a sacrifice. A sheep, goat, cow or camel is killed and the meat is shared with others.

Someone who has made the pilgrimage (Hajj) to Mecca

Isa Masih	Jesus the Messiah.
Islam	Literally means 'submission to God'. A Muslim is one who submits to God.
Jihad	Often regarded by the media as 'Holy War'. Some Muslims regard jihad as a literal physical struggle against unbelievers. Most Muslims view jihad as a personal struggle against one's evil inclinations.
Ka'aba	A cube-like shrine in the courtyard of the sacred mosque in Mecca towards which Muslims face during prayer.
Mosque	Literally 'place of prostration' (in prayer). The Muslim equivalent of a church building.
Muhammed	Founder of Islam, who was born in Mecca in 570AD and who died in 632AD. He claimed that his first revelation from God came to him in a vision at the age of forty after six months of meditation in a cave just outside Mecca. His migration to Medina in 622AD marks the beginning of the Islamic calendar.
Qur'an	The Muslims' sacred book containing the revelations received by Muhammed over a period of 22 years. Muslims are warned to wash and purify themselves before touching the Qur'an and must not hold it below waist level, place any other book or object on it, or place it on the floor.
Ramadan	The month of fasting – the ninth month of the Islamic lunar year. Ramadan is a holy month, intended as a time of spiritual self-improvement.

Similarities and differences

There are areas of common ground that we share with our Muslim friends...

God There is one God who is creator and sustainer of the universe. He is infinite, all-knowing, all-powerful and the sovereign judge.

Jesus Jesus was sent from God and was without sin. He was born of a virgin. He healed the sick, raised the dead, and is coming back a second time.

Revelation God has revealed His will to human beings through the prophets.

Day of Judgement God will judge all men. Some will spend eternity in the presence of God in heaven. Others will spend eternity separated from God in hell.

Some areas in which we think differently…

These describe general beliefs of many Muslims. However, your Muslim friend may or may not hold these beliefs personally. If you discuss your differences with your Muslim friend, please make sure that you show them respect. Argument is rarely helpful or persuasive.

God God Himself cannot be known, only His will can be known. God is greater than all man's ideas of Him. He has absolute power to do as He wills, and He predestines everything, both good and evil. Putting anyone or anything on the same level as God is unforgiveable sin (shirk).

Jesus Jesus was an exceptional messenger of God but not the Son of God. For God to become man is unthinkable. Muslims also believe God would never have abandoned so great a prophet as Jesus to human executioners.

The Scriptures The Old and New Testament Scriptures have been corrupted over the centuries and are no longer reliable. The Qur'an is God's final revelation and supersedes all other Scripture.

Salvation On the day of judgement, God will weigh each man's good deeds against his bad deeds to decide his eternal destiny. God has the absolute right to send individuals to paradise or hell as He chooses. Muslims can never be sure whether or not they will reach paradise. Most expect to spend some time being punished for their sins.

Forgiveness of sin There is no need for a penalty to be paid for sin. God merely forgives those who obey His commands.

Further common misunderstandings that often distract Muslims and turn them away from considering the gospel:

Most Muslims believe:

1. That Christians believe in three gods not one. Some Muslims think that the Christian trinity consists of God, Mary and Jesus, their son who resulted from their physical intercourse.

2. That Christians are committing *shirk* – the unpardonable sin of equating another being with God – when they say, 'Jesus is the Son of God.'

3. That Jesus was not crucified on the cross but was taken up to heaven. Someone, possibly Judas, is believed to have died in His place. Jesus is waiting to return a second time to tell the whole world that Islam is the true and final religion.

4. That Christians only have to go to church on Sundays and have no other religious duties.

Be aware that the word 'Christian' has a lot of cultural baggage to a Muslim. It was Christians who carried out the Crusades against Muslims. They also perceive that everyone born in the West is a Christian, including all pop stars, film stars and others in the media. For this reason, the term 'follower of Jesus' may more accurately convey to a Muslim who you really are.

10

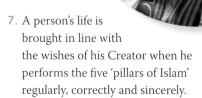

Some additional insights into the beliefs and practices of our Muslim friends:

Muslims believe that:

1. God is the sole source of power and authority, so He is entitled to worship and obedience from human beings.

2. Islam is a way of life based on total obedience to God, from whom everything originates and who is the creator, sustainer and only source of guidance.

3. God has given guidance to mankind about how we should live. This guidance was sent down to various prophets but when people distorted it, God sent another prophet to bring human beings back to the 'straight path'.

4. The final guidance was given in the Qur'an which came to Muhammed. The Qur'an has existed for ever in Arabic on golden tablets in paradise.

5. Every person must work to establish the laws of the Creator in all areas of their life in order to gain God's pleasure.

6. Every person will be judged on their actions, each of which is being recorded by an angel. If we obey the will of God, we will be rewarded with a place of happiness in paradise. If not, we will be punished in hell.

7. A person's life is brought in line with the wishes of his Creator when he performs the five 'pillars of Islam' regularly, correctly and sincerely.

8. Reciting the Qur'an is one way of communing with God. Thus memorising it and reciting it are very important.

9. Muhammed is a model for everything in life.

Communicating God's love to Muslims

Some general points on how to introduce Muslims to Jesus:

• Love Muslims sincerely and caringly, with a Christ-like love. The aim is not to defend Christianity but to present Jesus.

• In the context of your genuine friendship, be open about your love for God. Most Muslims are very willing to talk about spiritual topics. Let your friend know that God is interested in his or her needs or concerns and offer to pray or read relevant Bible passages.

• When it's appropriate, talk about how you found peace and assurance of salvation through Christ. No-one can argue with your testimony.

• Listen patiently to what your friend says so that you will understand him or her better. Your turn will come to talk, and it is important to speak to their needs and concerns instead of giving a standard presentation. Most people need to hear the good news about Jesus' love for them many times before they comprehend it.

• Study the culture and ways of thinking of Muslims. In many cultures, one makes a point by illustration. It may be helpful for you to build up a supply of suitable stories to illustrate various points.

• Ask God to help you direct the conversation to spiritual issues when it's appropriate. Many Muslims concentrate on the outward differences of religious practice, such as postures while praying.

• Stress that God is a heavenly Father and that everyone can have a personal relationship with Him as His child.

• Stress the unique being of Jesus Christ:
   a. His miraculous birth and the prophecies concerning His birth.
   b. His sinless life and extraordinary teaching.
   c. His unique names (the Qur'an calls Him 'the Word of God' and 'a Spirit of God').
   d. The fact that He is alive.
   e. The fact that He is returning.

Love Muslims sincerely and caringly, with a Christ-like love

- Explain the good news very simply.

- Encourage Muslims to read the Bible for themselves, especially the Gospels. The Sermon on the Mount and some of the parables often speak very clearly to them. In fact the Qur'an encourages Muslims to read God's Word:

    Surah 3:84 – 'You must believe the Bible'

    Surah 2:46 – 'The Bible and Qur'an are of divine origin'

    Surah 10:95 – 'Consult the other Scriptures'

- Make a distinction between true and nominal Christians. Point out that not everyone who calls himself a Christian is truly following Jesus Christ.

- Realise that politics and religion are closely linked in Islam. Instead of arguing about politics, explain how your relationship with Jesus affects your life.

- Avoid arguing – answer objections with gentleness and kindness.

- Your Muslim friend will likely be curious about your attitude toward Muhammed. Your response should be honest without causing needless offense to your friend.

- Don't assume that words have the same meaning. To a Muslim:

    a. Sin refers to something declared unlawful, not evil itself.

    b. Prayer means a ritual performed five times a day.

    c. Sonship means that Jesus Christ is Son of God in a physical sense.

    d. Faith means believing the Muslim creed.

    e. Heaven (ie paradise) is thought of as a place of sensual pleasures by many Muslims.

Further helpful points to bear in mind

• Show respect to books Muslims consider to be holy (the Bible and Qur'an). While carrying or handling the Bible or New Testament, hold it above your waist. Never put it on the floor. When showing a Bible to a Muslim, try to use one which has not been marked or highlighted.

• Be ready to stand or kneel when praying, as these are more normal prayer postures for a Muslim. If you do sit, don't cross your legs as that is considered disrespectful toward God.

• Speak of Jesus as 'Isa Masih' or 'The Lord Jesus Christ'. It is disrespectful not to give Jesus a title.

• Feel free to express your genuine sadness at the state of Western society and morals.

• Remember that pork and alcohol (and sometimes dogs) are considered 'dirty' by Muslims.

• Avoid eating in front of a Muslim during the hours of fasting in the month of Ramadan unless he is eating too.

• Dress in a modest way. Ensure your body is appropriately covered. Ask your Muslim friend how a godly person would dress.

• Don't show the bottom of your feet and don't use your left hand to eat or to offer things to people, as both are considered 'unclean' in many cultures.

• Most Muslims come from societies where the role of the sexes and interaction between men and women outside the family are more restricted than in the West. Therefore it is usually appropriate for men to relate to men and women to women. Don't shake hands with someone of the opposite sex unless the other person initiates it. You may be invited to a home and find that family members of the opposite sex are nowhere to be seen!

- When talking about spiritual things, it may be best to use stories, personal illustrations of faith and parables as much as possible. Most people, including Muslims, are not usually impressed by logical reasons for faith.

- Your Muslim friend will usually be pleased if you offer to pray to Isa Masih (Jesus Christ) for them. If appropriate, you may want to let your friend know that they can ask Jesus for help directly, praying in His name.

- The 'Jesus' film on the life of Christ from Luke's Gospel often speaks powerfully. It is available in many languages at www.jesusfilm.org. You may also be able to obtain an English copy through your local Christian bookshop.

- Your Muslim friend may be very legalistic. Stories told by Jesus about the importance of the heart can really speak to them eg Luke 18:9-14. Emphasise the fact that we can know God and have a growing relationship with Him.

- In general, communicate Christ with friends of the same gender – men to men and women to women.

- Invite several friends to a discussion on, say, 'How to find true peace' or 'The secret of happiness' or 'Principles for living' or 'The coming Day of Judgement'. Other popular topics: 'What is Heaven like?', 'How will we recognise the last days?', 'The life and teachings of Isa Masih', 'God's most important commands' and 'How to get God's help'. It would probably be most appropriate to hold separate events for men and women.

- When appropriate, you can share that through Isa Masih it is possible to receive forgiveness of sins.

- Talk about how the Bible helps us with guidelines on:

    a. relationships with other people and particularly how love can overcome resentment and bitterness.

    b. wife – husband relations

    c. how to bring up children

    d. other relevant day-to-day practical issues

Emphasise the fact that we can know God and have a growing relationship with Him

Sharing Christ with Muslim Women

*Some cultural aspects
to bear in mind*

When with Muslim women, you can show your consideration for their culture by being conservative in how you dress (eg no short skirts, shorts, or sleeveless tops), unless they themselves dress in a modern way. If uncertain about what to wear, you could ask your Muslim friend what a godly woman would usually wear.

Bear in mind that many Muslim women prefer not to go out alone, even during the day. Also many women would not visit the women of the household if the husband were present.

Some very conservative Muslim women are not used to making decisions and will hold back from doing so because their fathers or brothers normally decide for them.

Muslim women are often steeped in folk Islam. At times of illness or bereavement or when they are barren and wanting children, they turn to Muslim holy men who will pray over them and give them charms to wear. Ask God for opportunities to pray for them and to share that Jesus is the most powerful of all holy men, the one mediator between God and man.

Use stories,

personal

illustrations

of faith and

parables

You could have a Bible-reading afternoon when a number of women are invited to hear teachings of Christ or watch the Jesus video, followed by tea. Remember that hospitality is central to Muslim culture, but be sensitive about halal requirements.

Some suggested questions to ask

Muslims are often much more open to talking about spiritual things than we are in the West. Here are a few questions you could ask. Take time to listen to their response and to hear their heart.

- How much do you think about God? What do you think He is like?

- How do you worship God?

- Do you know God as a loving Father in a personal way?

- If you were to die today, would you go to heaven or not?

- What is the way a Muslim gets to heaven?

- Do you know whether or not your sins are forgiven?

- Do you have eternal life?

- What can overcome the power that makes us all sin?

- What do you think of the Lord Jesus Christ?

- Have you read any of the teachings of the Lord Jesus Christ?

- Have you read His life story?

- Do you know the difference between a true Christian and someone born in a 'Christian' country?

Adapted from an article written by Shamshad Ali, an Indian Muslim convert.

Replying to Questions

There are some common questions that Muslims ask us. Think through these questions and personalise the responses using your own words.

1. Why do Christians eat pork?

Do you know what Isa Masih said about eating unclean food? 'It is not what goes into the mouth that defiles it, but what comes out... What comes out of the mouth comes from the heart.'

2. Do you pray [ie perform the ritual prayers five times a day]?

I talk to God many times a day, and He answers me...

But do you cleanse yourself [ie by ritual washing] before you pray?

I ask Isa Masih to cleanse my heart before I talk to God – for He spoke against those who clean the outside of the cup but inside are full of wickedness. When our hearts are clean, then God will hear us.

3. Why don't you become a Muslim?

I am a follower of Isa Masih – the Word of God in human form. He is showing me the way to God. He gave the most amazing moral teaching. He has freed me from the powers of evil and from the power of sin in my life.

4. How can God have a Son?

Reply with a question – 'what do you mean by 'Son of God'? If your friend replies that they think this means God had sex with Mary, you can agree with them that this idea is blasphemous. He is the Word of God in human form (read the first part of the book of John in the Injil). When we look at Jesus and see how He lived and hear His words, explain that we can know what God's nature is like.

5. How could God allow one of His prophets to be killed on a cross?

Isa Masih said, 'My blood ... is poured out for many for the forgiveness of sins.' He showed that His whole aim in coming to earth was in a rescue mission to save men and women from the consequences of their sins.

Further reading

This booklet has given a brief introduction to sharing Christ with Muslims. Other books available that will help you to build upon what you have learnt here include:

Friendship First by Steve Bell. A practical and easy-to-read handbook providing many insights into ordinary Christians sharing the good news about Jesus with ordinary Muslims.

Islam and Christian Witness by Martin Goldsmith. An excellent short introduction to Islam with insights on how Christians can explain the gospel to Muslims.

Faith to Faith by Chawkat Moucarry. A study on Christianity and Islam in dialogue.

Encountering the World of Islam edited by Keith Swartley. A comprehensive collection of articles from over eighty authors, providing a positive, balanced and Biblical perspective on God's heart for Muslims and equipping you to reach out to them in Christ's love.

Muslims, Magic and the Kingdom of God by Rick Love. Folk Islam practices feature strongly in the lives of many Muslims. Rick Love draws from 20 years experience of working with Muslims, bringing Biblical perspectives and hope for introducing Christ to Muslims who are heavily influenced by Folk Islam.

Daughters of Islam by Miriam Adeney. Ten per cent of the world's population are Muslim women and they live throughout the earth. This book shares about their lives, questions and hopes, and gives many practical tips to help us relate to Muslim women in our own neighbourhood and workplace.

The Bible and the Qur'an: A Question of Integrity by Stephen Masood. This book deals with frequently raised differences between these two holy books.

Into the Light by Stephen Masood. A Muslim man shares his story of how his life has been changed through an encounter with Jesus.

I Dared to Call Him Father by Bilquis Sheikh. A Muslim woman shares how she came to know the love of her heavenly Father.

Prayer Guides – available for different people groups and nations.

All these books are available from the Frontiers Office. For further resources and new titles, go to www.frontiers.org.uk and click on the resources page.

Other resources
Jesus video – available in many languages. www.jesusfilm.org

For Christian resources available in Muslim languages see www.kitab.org.uk

How to Get Involved in the Muslim World

- Find out how you can get involved in introducing Jesus to Muslims in your area.

- Commit yourself to pray regularly for individuals who are living in Muslim communities and seeking to share Christ's love.

- Suggest to your church, house group or Christian Union that they focus on particular Muslim communities which still do not have followers of Jesus among them.

- Pray about getting a team together to go and work in the Muslim world.

- Join with others who are communicating the good news of Jesus in the Muslim World. We can talk to you about opportunities in more than 40 countries.

About 1.3 billion, or one in five of the world's population, are Muslims. Very few have heard the good news about Jesus. The map below shows the location of Muslims throughout the world. Do pray for many more followers of Jesus to take His love to those who have not yet heard.

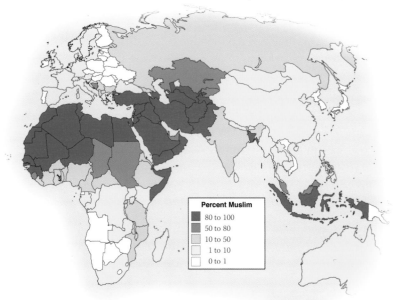

Percent Muslim
- 80 to 100
- 50 to 80
- 10 to 50
- 1 to 10
- 0 to 1

Information about Frontiers

Frontiers was formed over 20 years ago in the belief that God uses ordinary people to achieve His purposes in extraordinary ways. Teams of like-minded people take their professions, gifts and dreams and live out the love of God in Muslim communities. Their desire is to see groups of Muslims come to know and follow Jesus, and indigenous leaders trained up, resulting in groups that flourish and multiply. Frontiers works in partnership with local churches here in the UK to prepare and enable such teams to serve people throughout the Muslim world who don't yet know Jesus.

See our website for further information: www.frontiers.org.uk.

Map on page 20 © Global Mapping International

Layout: www.jacdesign.co.uk

1st edition ©1994 Frontiers, England
2nd revised edition ©2001 Frontiers, England
3rd revised edition ©2006 Frontiers, England

Frontiers

Partnering to see
God's Kingdom come
in Muslim lives and communities

FRONTIERS
PO Box 1445
HIGH WYCOMBE
HP12 9BU
Tel: 0303 333 5051

Email: info@frontiers.org.uk

Website: www.frontiers.org.uk

ISBN 0-9542594-2-4